SCHIRMER'S LIBRARY
OF MUSICAL CLASSICS

Vol. 2136

35 SONATINAS
by 10 Composers

for Piano

Bartók, Beethoven, Clementi, Diabelli, Dussek,
Kuhlau, Lichner, Mozart, Reinecke, Spindler

ISBN 978-1-5400-1269-2

G. SCHIRMER, Inc.

DISTRIBUTED BY

7777 W. BLUEMOUND RD. P.O. BOX 13819 MILWAUKEE, WI 53213

CONTENTS

Sonatina

1. Bagpipe

Béla Bartók
Sz. 55

4

Allegro ($\quarternote$ = 140-150)

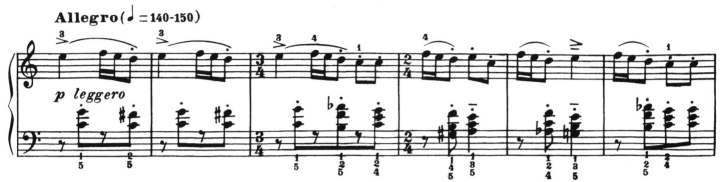

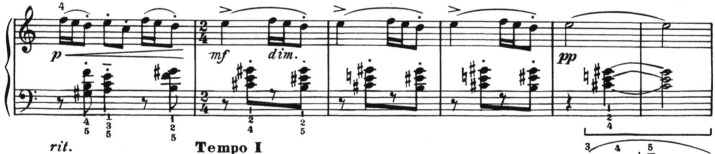

rit.   **Tempo I**

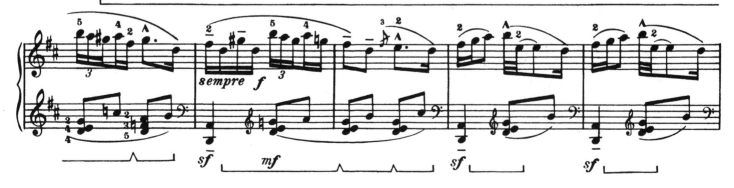

II. Dance*

* In the 1950 edition, Bartók retitled this movement, "Bear Dance."

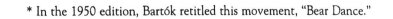

III. Finale

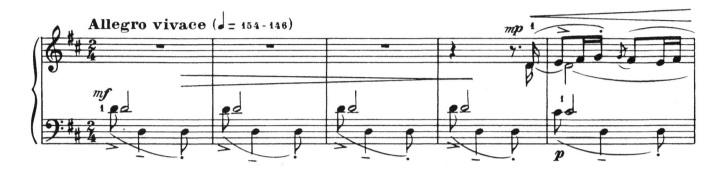

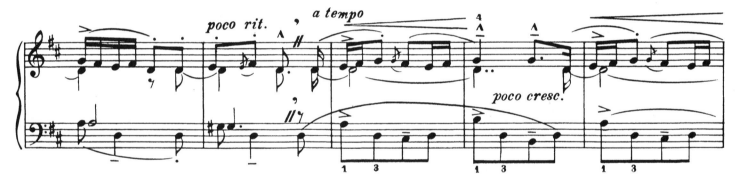

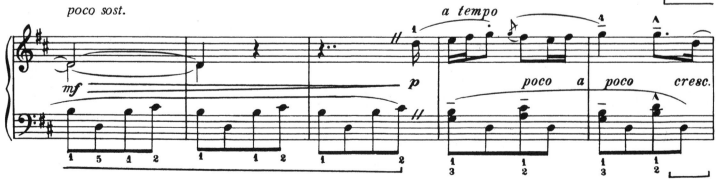

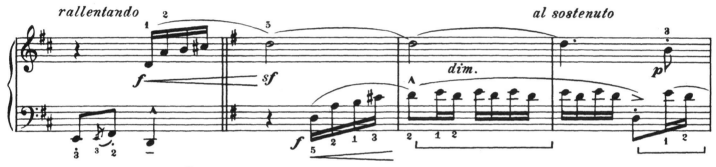

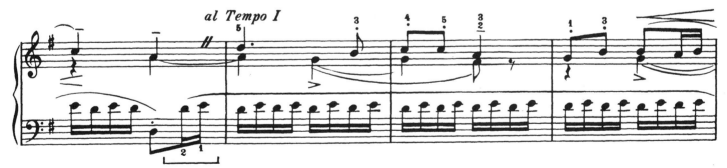

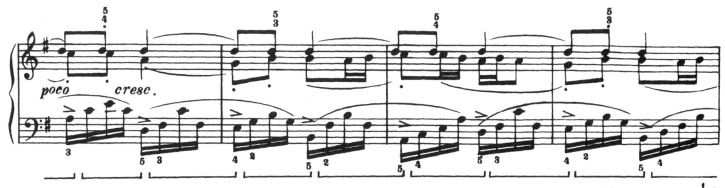

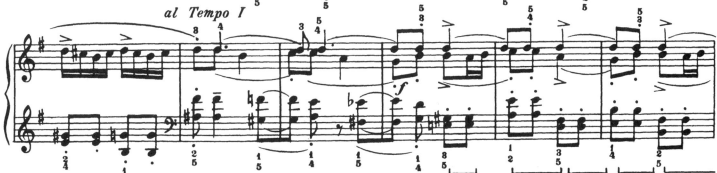

Sonatina in G Major

Ludwig van Beethoven
Anh. 5, No. 1

Moderato

ROMANZE

Sonatina in F Major

Ludwig van Beethoven
Anh. 5, No. 2

Allegro assai

RONDO
Allegro

Sonatina in C Major

Muzio Clementi
Op. 36, No. 1

Spiritoso

Andante

Vivace

Sonatina in G Major

Muzio Clementi
Op. 36, No. 2

Allegretto.

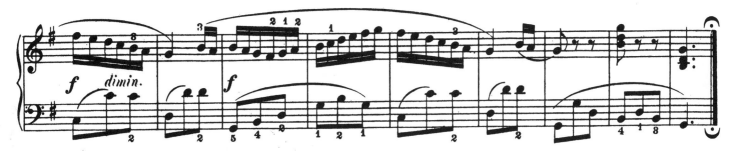

23

Sonatina in C Major

Muzio Clementi
Op. 36, No. 3

Spiritoso.

Sonatina in F Major

Muzio Clementi
Op. 36, No. 4

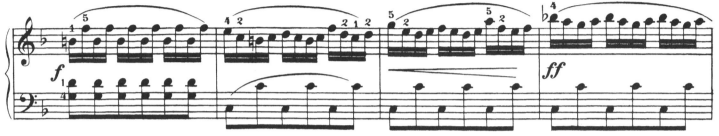

Andante con espressione

Rondo
Allegro vivace

Da Capo al Fine

Sonatina in G Major

Muzio Clementi
Op. 36, No. 5

Air Suisse (Original.)
Allegro moderato.

Rondo
Allegro di molto

Sonatina in D Major

Muzio Clementi
Op. 36, No. 6

Allegro con spirito.

44

Rondo.
Allegretto spiritoso

45

Sonatina in G Major

Anton Diabelli
Op. 151, No. 1

Andante cantabile.

Scherzo.

Allegro.

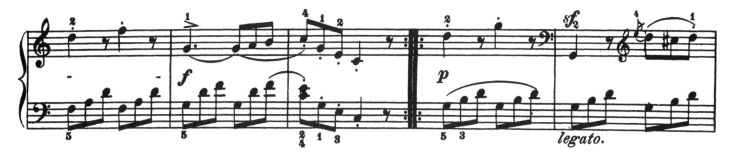

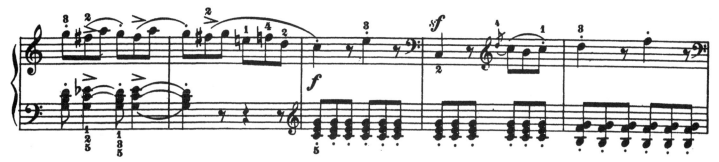

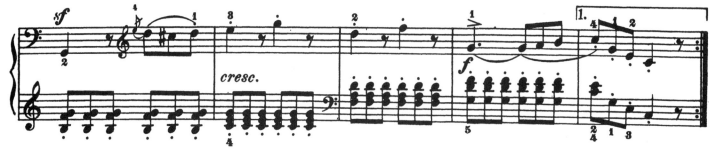

Rondo.
Allegretto.

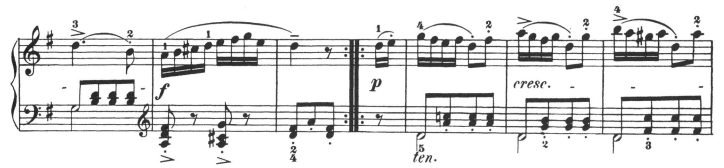

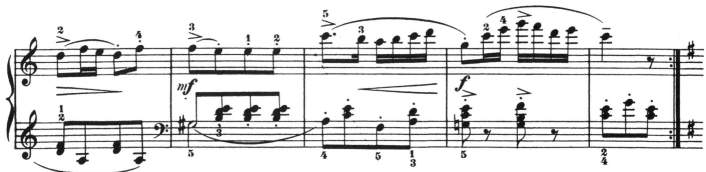

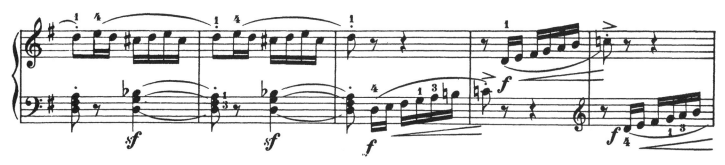

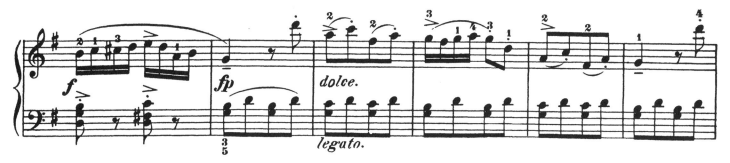

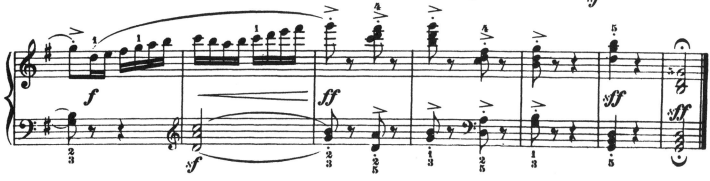

Sonatina in C Major

Anton Diabelli
Op. 151, No. 4

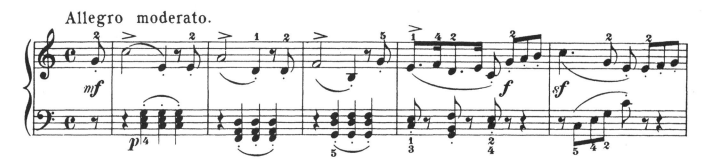

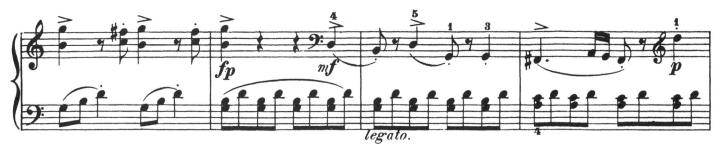

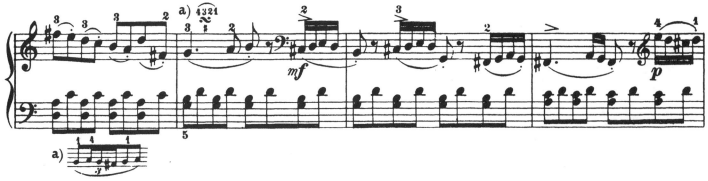

53

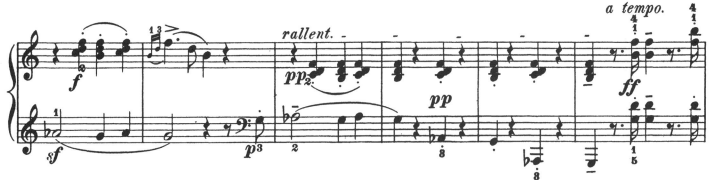

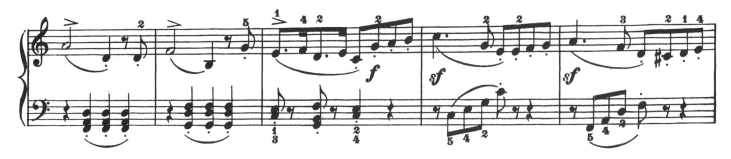

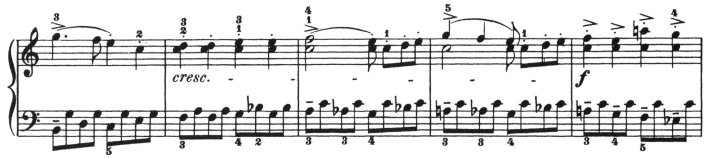

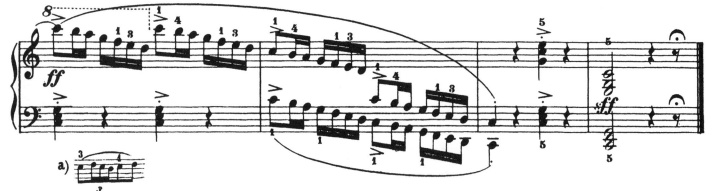

Introduction.
Largo maestoso.

Rondo.
Allegro ma non troppo.

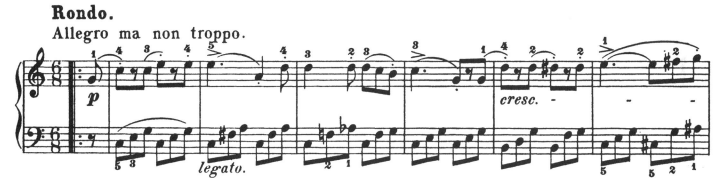

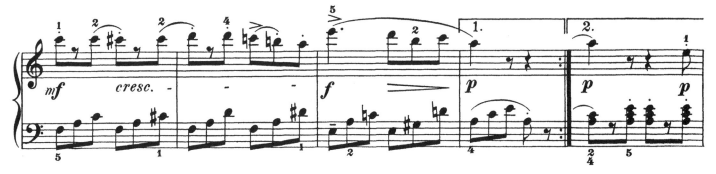

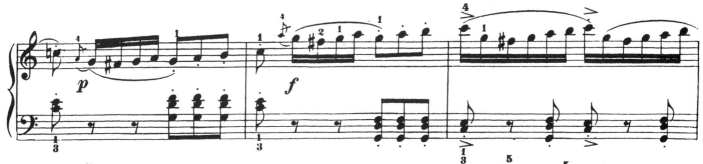

Sonatina in C Major

Anton Diabelli
Op. 168, No. 3

Allegro moderato

a)

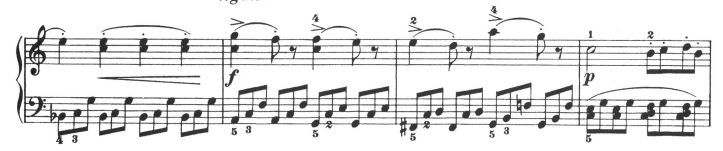

Andantino

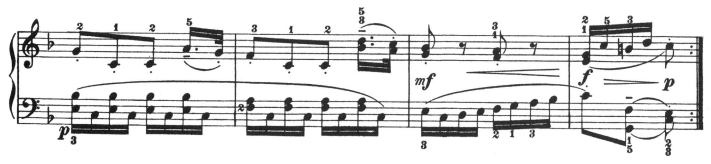

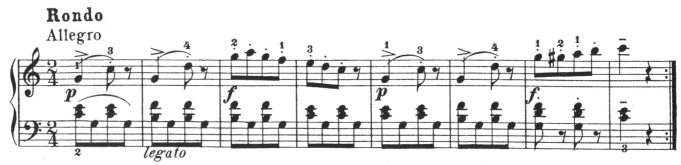

Rondo

Allegro

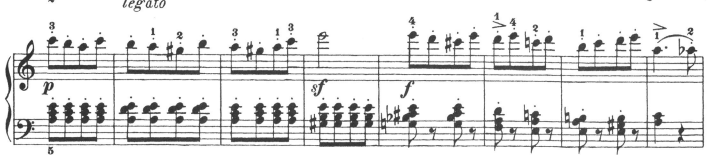

Sonatina in A minor

Anton Diabelli
Op. 168, No. 7

Tempo I.

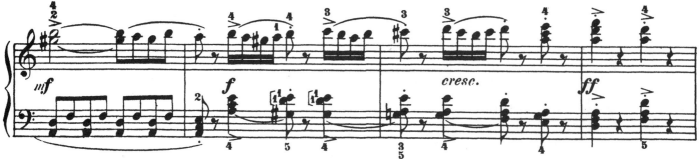

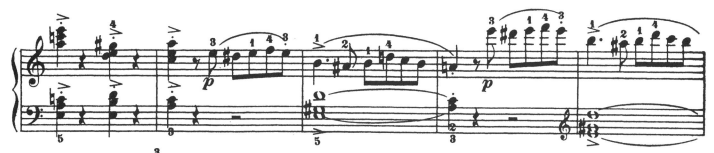

Andante cantabile.

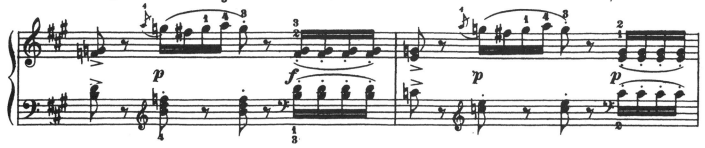

Rondo.
Allegretto.

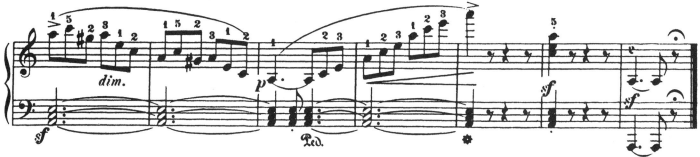

Sonatina in G Major

Jan Ladislav Dussek
Op. 20, No. 1

Allegro non tanto

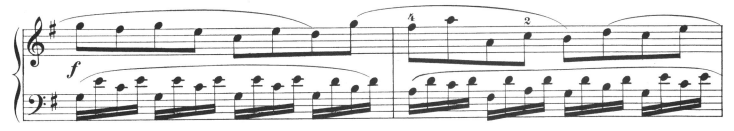

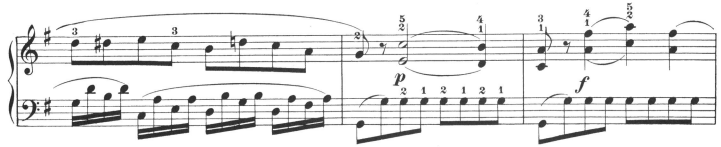

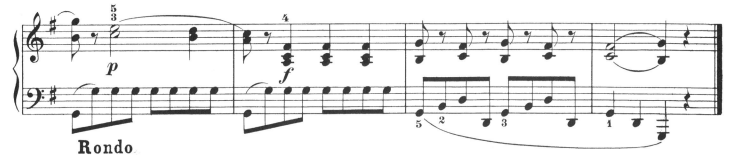

Rondo
Allegretto Tempo di Minuetto

Minore

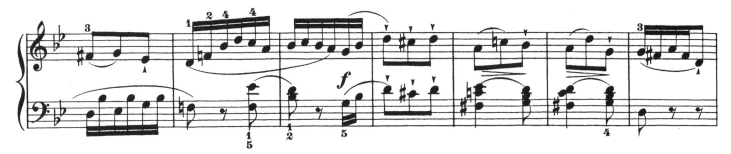

Maggiore

Sonatina in F Major

Jan Ladislav Dussek
Op. 20, No. 3

Allegro, quasi presto.

74

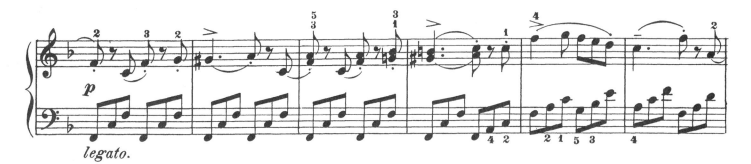

Rondo.

Andantino.

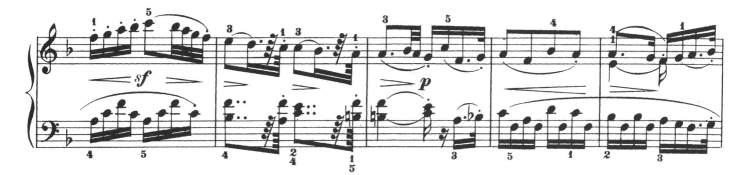

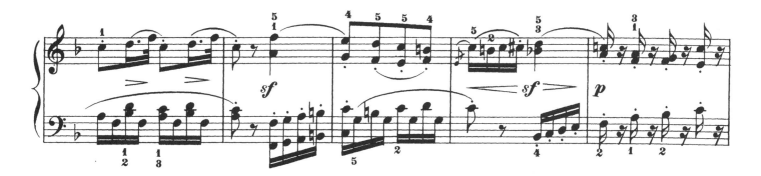

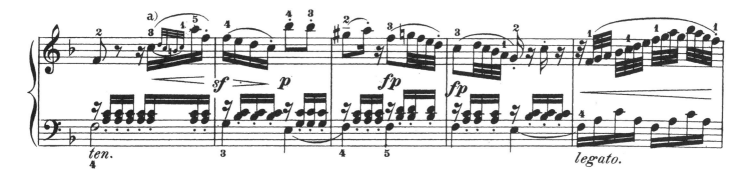

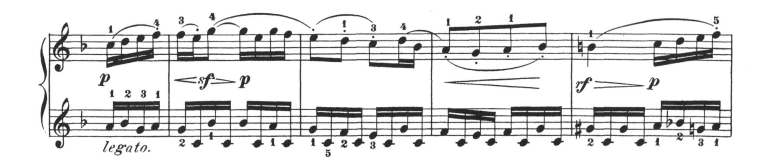

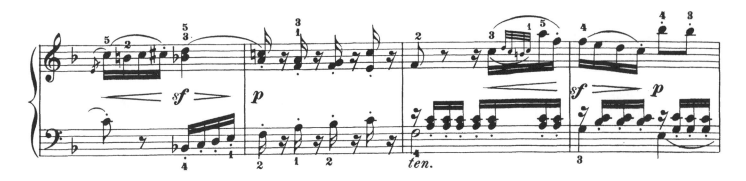

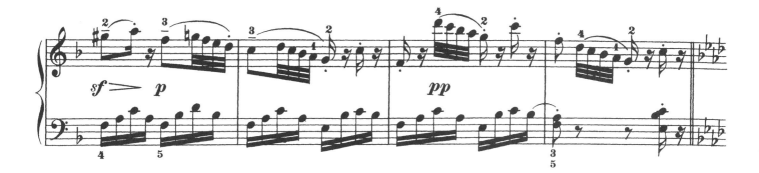

Minore.

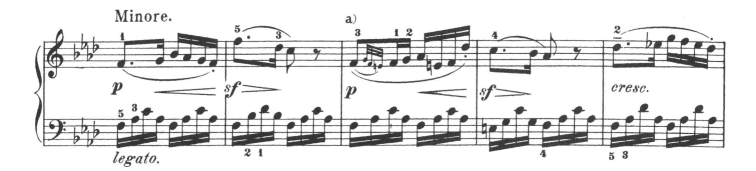

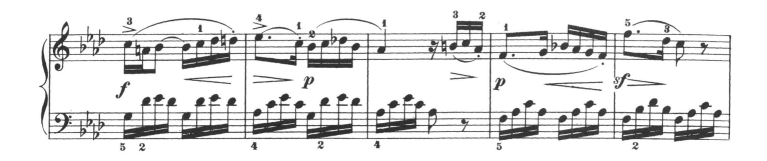

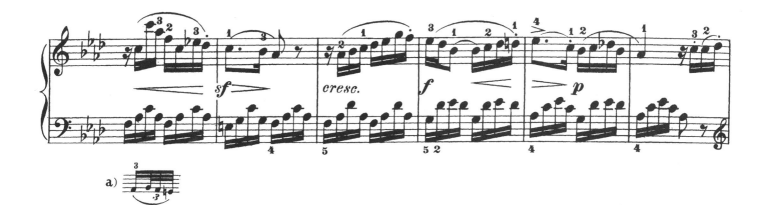

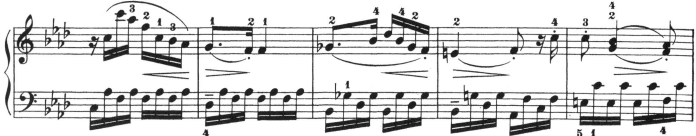

Maggiore.

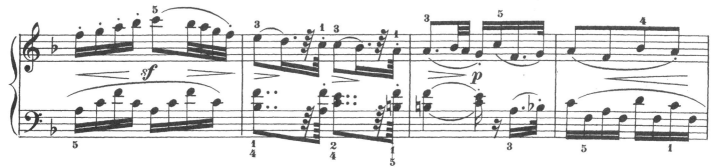

Sonatina in E-flat Major

Jan Ladislav Dussek
Op. 20, No. 6

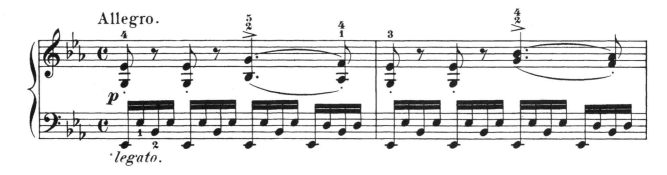

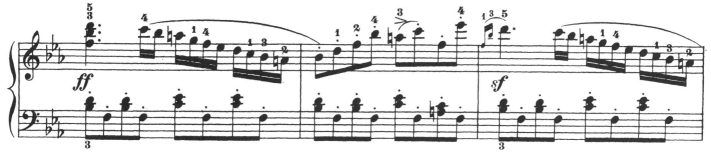

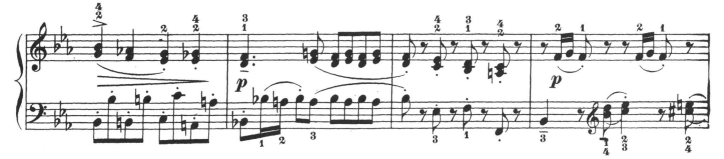

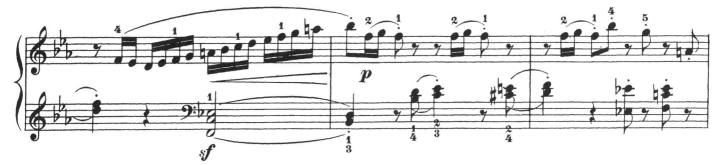

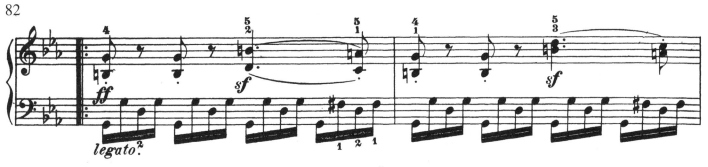

Allegretto.

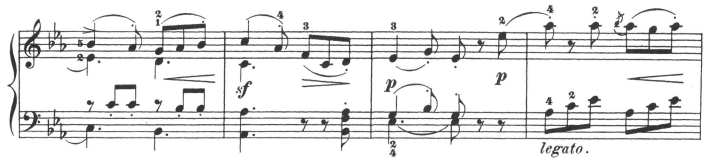

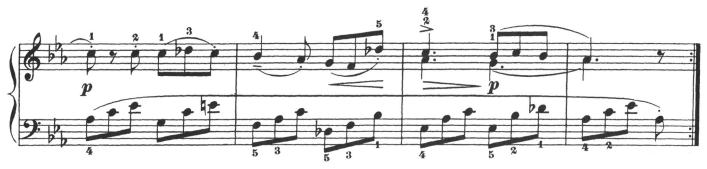

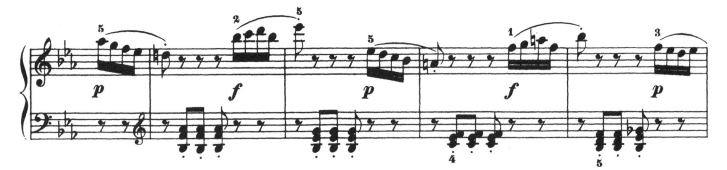

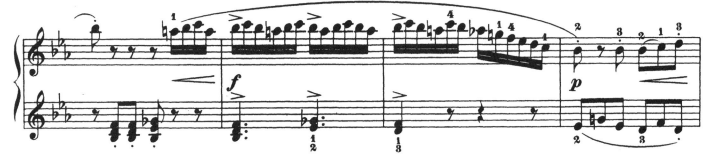

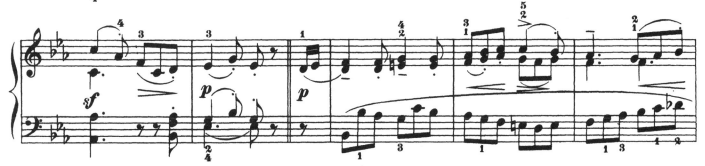

Sonatina in C Major

Friedrich Kuhlau
Op. 20, No. 1

a) These small slurs indicate that the last bass-note in one measure should be carefully connected with the first bass-note in the next.

Sonatina in G Major

Friedrich Kuhlau
Op. 20, No. 2

Adagio e sostenuto

Allegro scherzando

a) Strike the appoggiatura simultaneously with the accompaniment.

99

Sonatina in C Major

Friedrich Kuhlau
Op. 55, No. 1

*) These small slurs indicate that the last bass-note in one measure should be carefully connected with the first bass-note in the next.

Sonatina in G Major

Friedrich Kuhlau
Op. 55, No. 2

*) These small slurs indicate that the last bass-note in one measure should be carefully connected with the first bass-note in the next.

Sonatina in C Major

Friedrich Kuhlau
Op. 55, No. 3

Allegro con spirito

*) These small slurs indicate that the last bass-note in one measure should be carefully connected with the first bass-note in the next.

Allegretto grazioso

Sonatina in C Major

Heinrich Lichner
Op. 4, No. 1

Allegro moderato (♩ = 132)

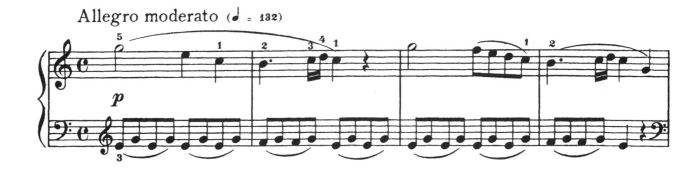

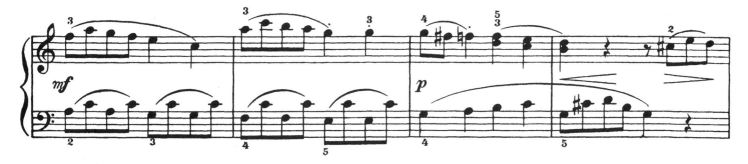

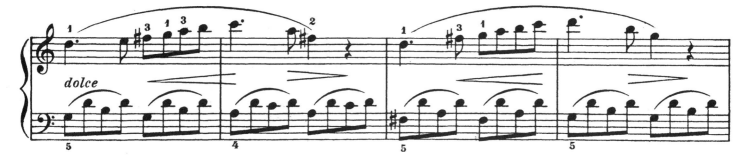

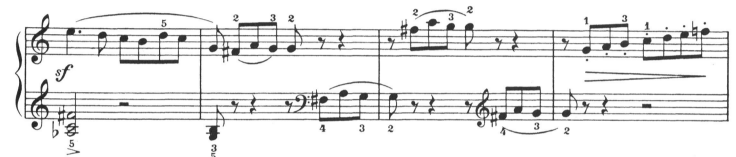

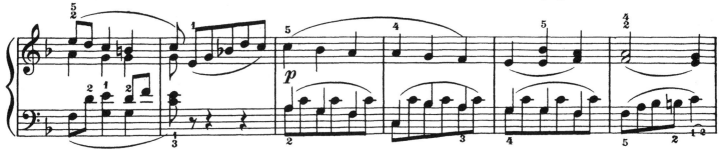

Andante cantabile (♩ = 184)

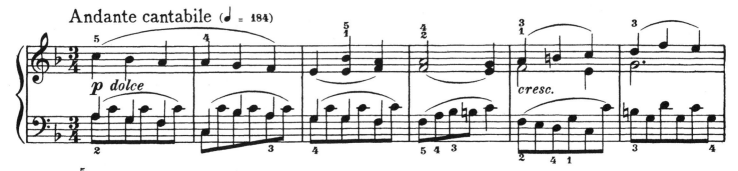

Rondo grazioso

Allegro (♩ = 112)

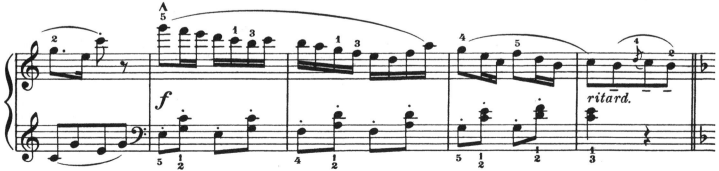

Sonatina in C Major

Heinrich Lichner
Op. 66, No. 1

Allegro moderato

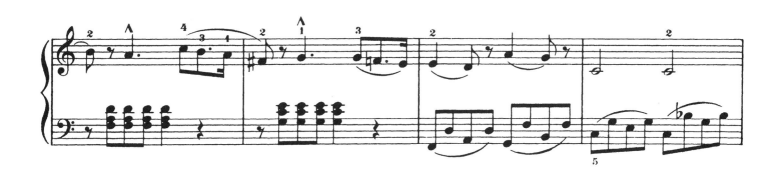

Andante

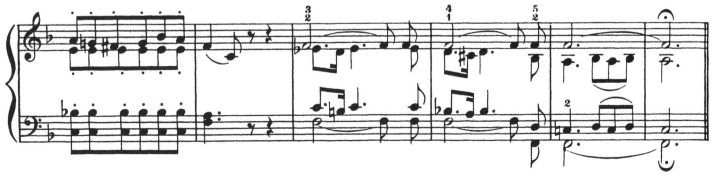

RONDO
Allegro ma non troppo

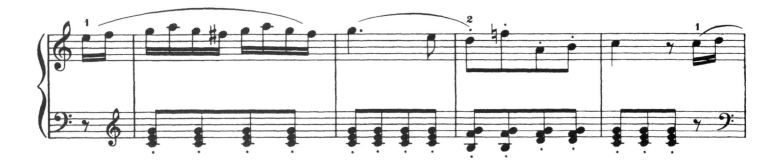

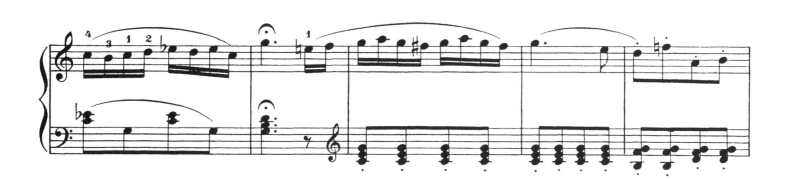

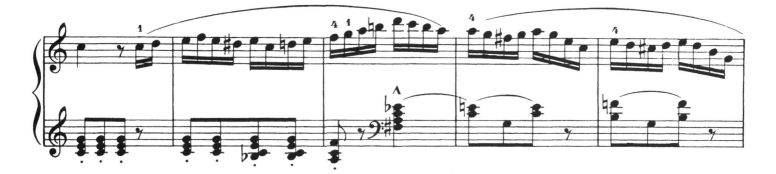

Sonatina in F Major

Heinrich Lichner
Op. 66, No. 2

Allegro moderato

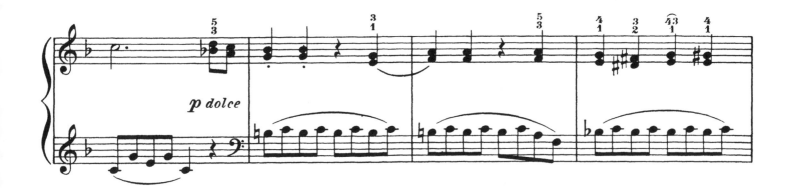

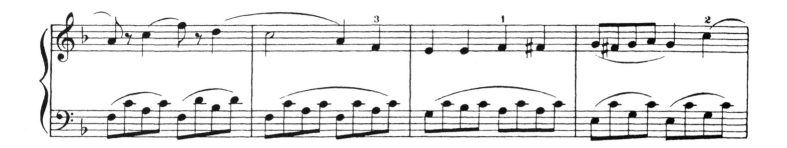

Andante cantabile

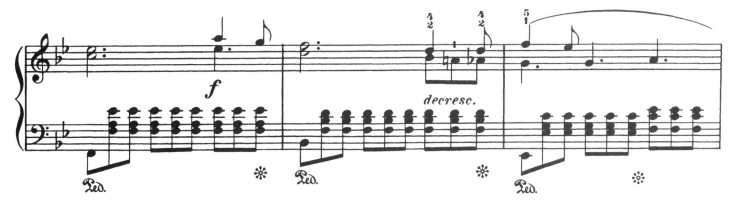

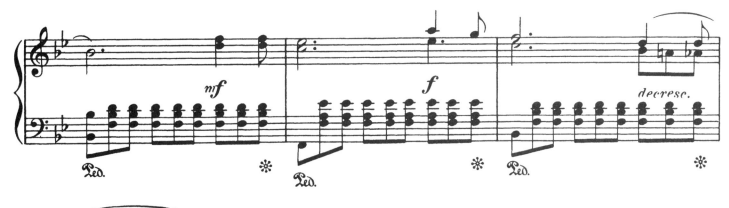

Moderato

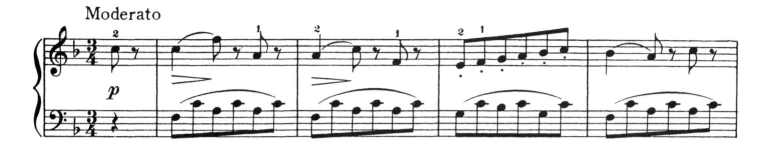

Sonatina in G Major

Heinrich Lichner
Op. 66, No. 3

Moderato

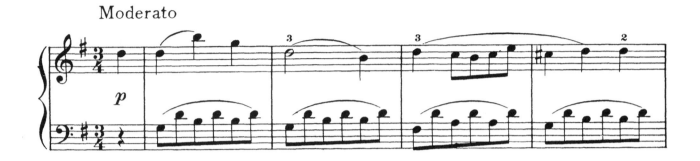

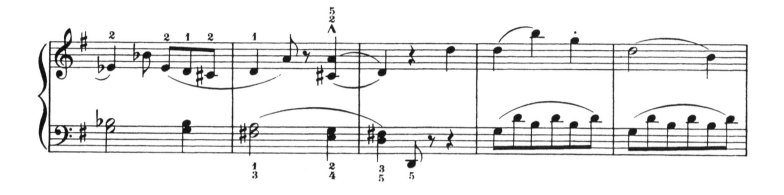

ROMANZE
Andantino

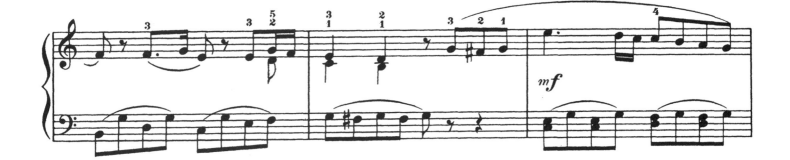

RONDO

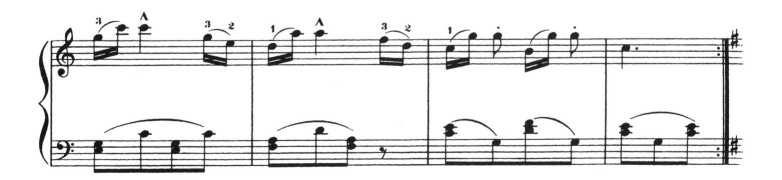

Sonatina No. 1 in C Major

from *Six Viennese Sonatinas*

Wolfgang Amadeus Mozart

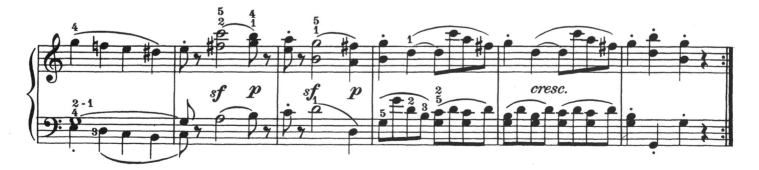

140

Ossia

Menuetto

Allegretto

Trio

Adagio

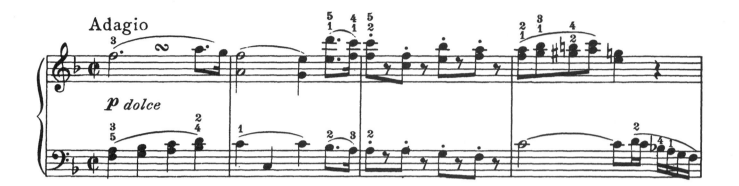

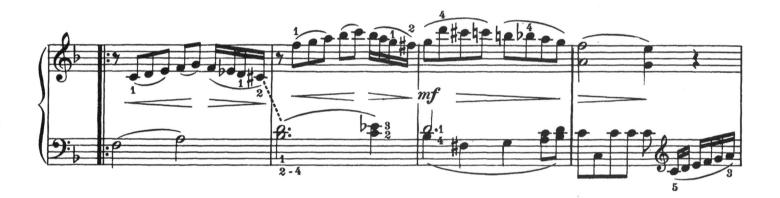

Rondo

Allegretto

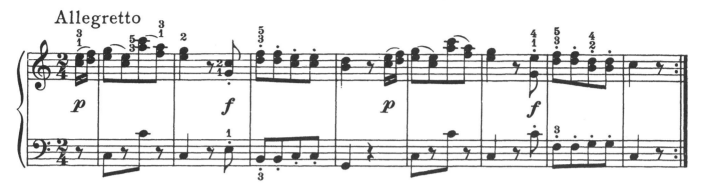

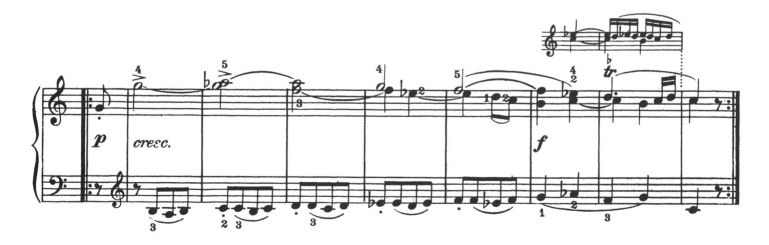

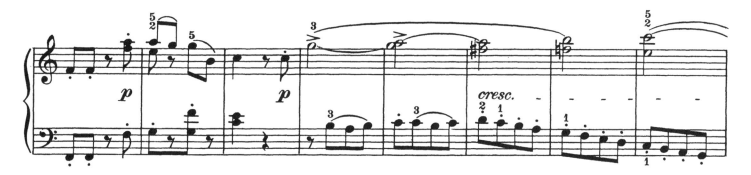

Sonatina No. 2 in A Major

from *Six Viennese Sonatinas*

Wolfgang Amadeus Mozart

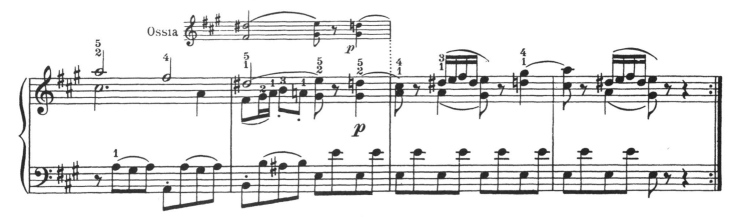

Menuetto

Allegretto

Trio

Ossia

Adagio

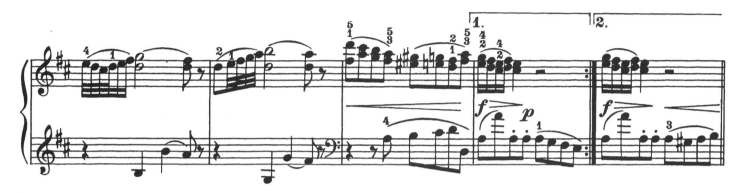

Rondo
Allegro

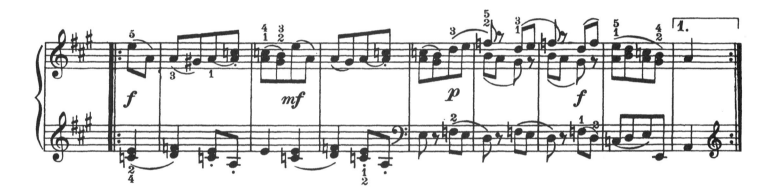

Ossia

Sonatina No. 3 in D Major

from *Six Viennese Sonatinas*

Wolfgang Amadeus Mozart

158

Rondo
Allegro

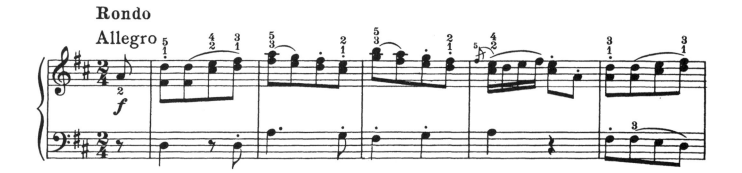

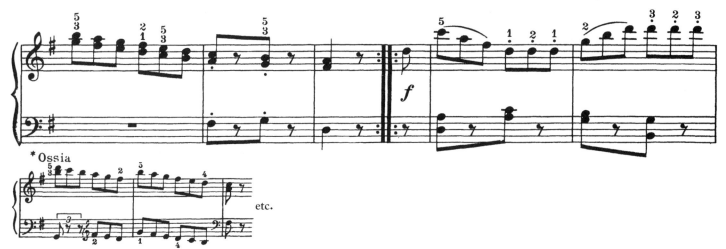

*Ossia

etc.

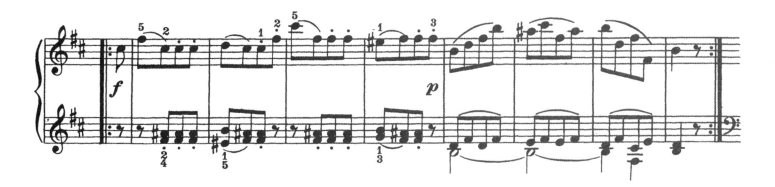

Sonatina No. 4 in B-flat Major

from *Six Viennese Sonatinas*

Wolfgang Amadeus Mozart

Romanze
Andante

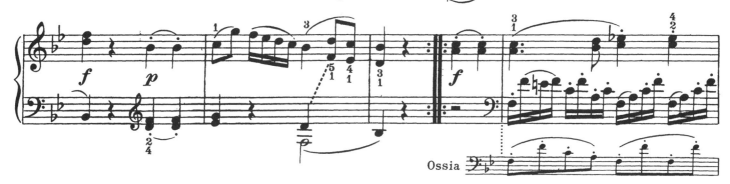

Menuetto
Allegretto

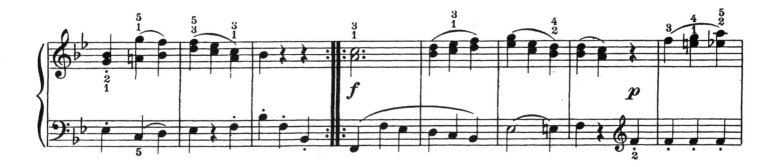

Trio

Menuetto da capo

Rondo

Allegro assai

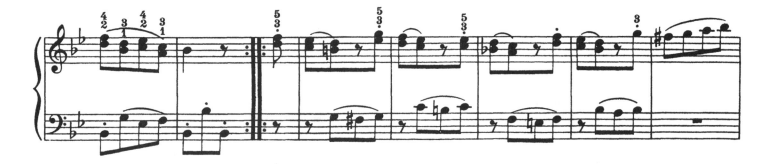

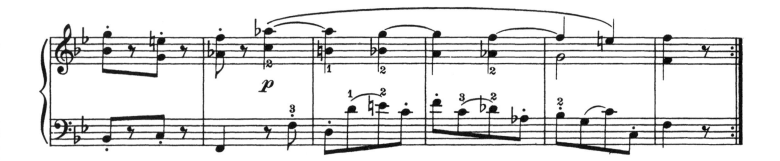

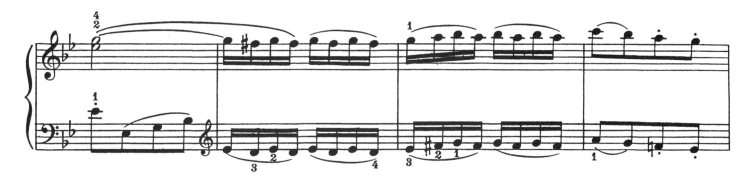

Sonatina No. 5 in F Major

from *Six Viennese Sonatinas*

Wolfgang Amadeus Mozart

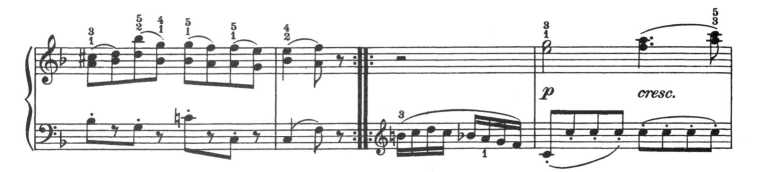

Menuetto

Allegretto

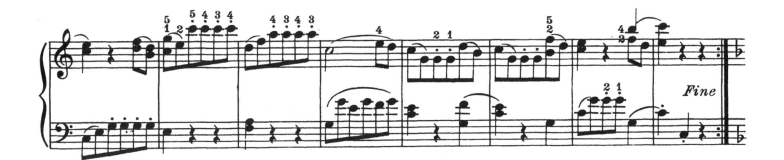

Trio

Polonaise

Sonatina No. 6 in C Major

from *Six Viennese Sonatinas*

Wolfgang Amadeus Mozart

Menuetto

Allegretto

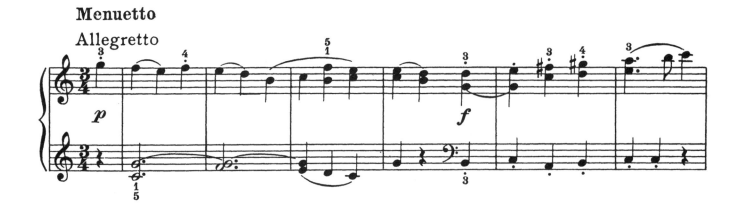

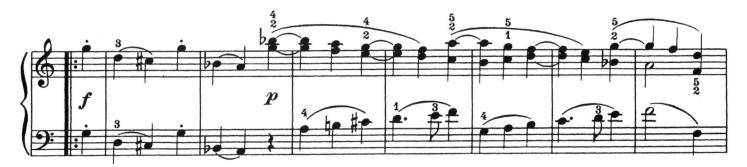

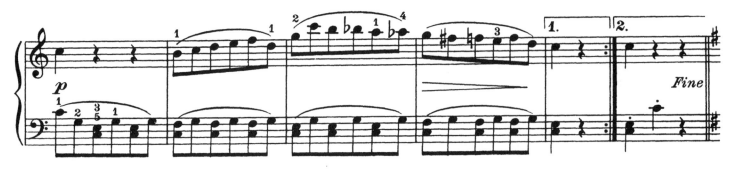

Trio

Menuetto da capo

Adagio

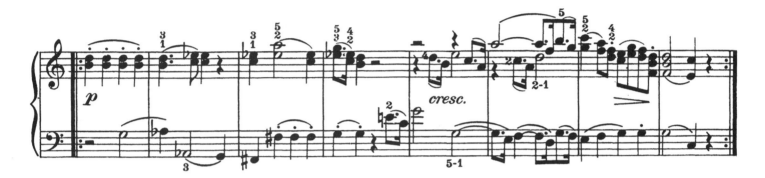

Finale

Allegro

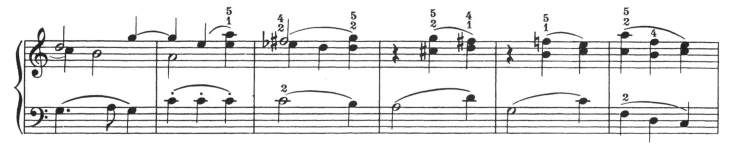

*Although F♯ may be played here, the original has F♮ at this point.

Sonatina in C Major

Carl Reinecke
Op. 136, No. 1

Allegretto

Primo Tempo

Scherzino
Vivace

Alla Polacca

Sonatina in G Major

Carl Reinecke
Op. 136, No. 2

Allegro moderato

Menuetto

Rondino
Vivace

Sonatina in C Major

Fritz Spindler
Op. 157, No. 4

Moderato.

Vivo.

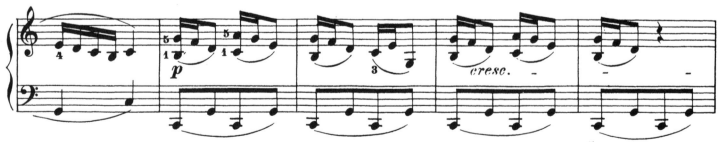

Sonatina in E minor

Fritz Spindler
Op. 157, No. 8

Allegretto con espressione ($\quarternote$ = 168)

194

Evening Song

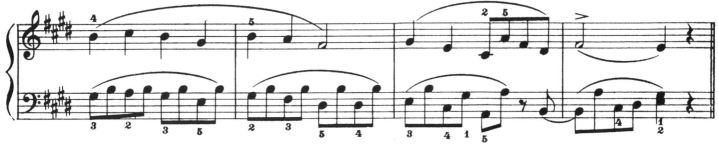

Allegro con fuoco (♩ = 152)

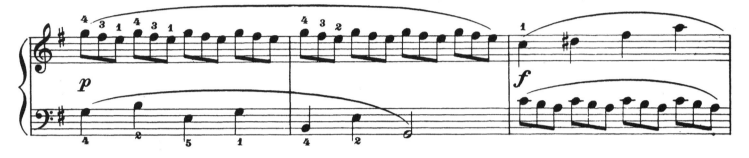

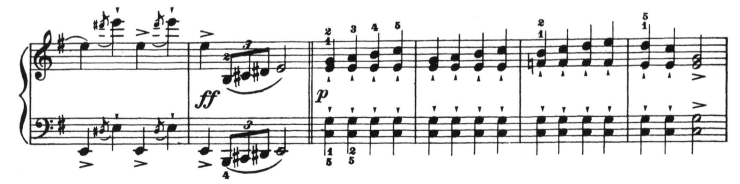